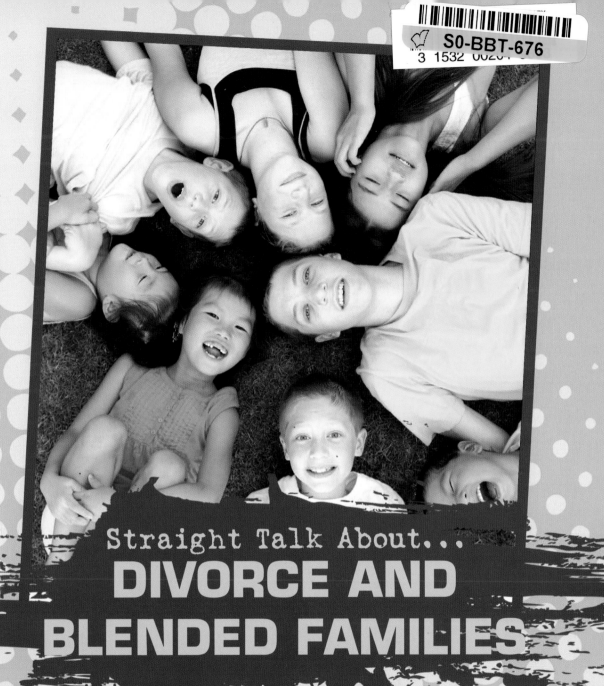

Straight Talk About...
DIVORCE AND BLENDED FAMILIES

Carrie Iorizzo

Crabtree Publishing Company
www.crabtreebooks.com

Straight Talk About...

Developed and produced by: Netscribes Inc.

Author: Carrie Iorizzo

Publishing plan research and development:
 Sean Charlebois, Reagan Miller
 Crabtree Publishing Company

Project Controller: Sandeep Kumar G

Editorial director: Kathy Middleton

Editors: John Perritano, Molly Aloian

Proofreader: Kelly McNiven

Art director: Dibakar Acharjee

Designer: Shruti Aggarwal

Cover design: Margaret Amy Salter

Production coordinator and
 prepress technician: Margaret Amy Salter

Print coordinators: Katherine Berti,
 Margaret Amy Salter

Consultant: Susan Cooper, M.Ed.

Photographs:
Cover: © Bubbles Photolibrary/Alamy; Title page:
amahuron/Shutterstock Inc.;p.4:David Davis/
Shutterstock Inc.; p.6:Rob Marmion/Shutterstock Inc.;
p.8:ejwhite/Shutterstock Inc.; p.9:Christo/
Shutterstock Inc.; p.10:ejwhite/Shutterstock Inc.;
p.11:Andy Dean Photography/Shutterstock Inc.;
p.12:CREATISTA/Shutterstock Inc.; p.14:Rob
Marmion/Shutterstock Inc.; p.15:Zoreslava/
Shutterstock Inc.; p.16:spotmatik/Shutterstock Inc.;
p.18:alexnika/Shutterstock Inc.; p.20:altanaka/
Shutterstock Inc.; p.21:iconogenic/Istockphoto.com;
p.22:Monkey Business Images/Shutterstock Inc.;
p.24:Sebastian Gauert/Shutterstock Inc.; p.25:Tracy
Whiteside/Shutterstock Inc.; p.26:Lisa Marzano/
Istockphoto.com; p.28:Oscar C. Williams/Shutterstock
Inc.; p.30:CREATISTA/Shutterstock Inc.; p.32:
michaeljung/Shutterstock Inc.; p.34:Goodluz/
Shutterstock Inc.; p.35:Blend Images/Shutterstock Inc.;
p.36:Rob Marmion/Shutterstock Inc.; p.39:Blend
Images/Shutterstock Inc.; p.40:auremar/Shutterstock
Inc.;p.41:Gladskikh Tatiana/Shutterstock Inc.;
p.42:Rob Marmion/Shutterstock Inc.

Library and Archives Canada Cataloguing in Publication

Iorizzo, Carrie
 Divorce and blended families / Carrie Iorizzo.

(Straight talk about--)
Includes index.
Issued also in electronic format.
ISBN 978-0-7787-2182-6 (bound).--ISBN 978-0-7787-2189-5 (pbk.)

 1. Divorce--Juvenile literature. 2. Remarriage--Juvenile
literature. 3. Stepfamilies--Juvenile literature. I. Title. II. Series:
Straight talk about-- (St. Catharines, Ont.)

HQ814.I67 2013   j306.89   C2013-901014-9

Library of Congress Cataloging-in-Publication Data

Iorizzo, Carrie.
 Divorce and blended families / Carrie Iorizzo.
  pages cm. -- (Straight talk about...)
 Includes index.
 Audience: Grade 4 to 6.
 ISBN 978-0-7787-2182-6 (reinforced library binding) --
ISBN 978-0-7787-2189-5 (pbk.) -- ISBN 978-1-4271-9065-9
(electronic pdf) -- ISBN 978-1-4271-9119-9 (electronic html)
 1. Divorce--Juvenile literature. 2. Children of divorced parents--
Juvenile literature. 3. Stepfamilies--Juvenile literature. I. Title.

 HQ814.I57 2013
 306.89--dc23
                        2013004904

Crabtree Publishing Company

www.crabtreebooks.com   1-800-387-7650

Printed in the USA/052013/JA20130412

Published in Canada
Crabtree Publishing
616 Welland Ave.
St. Catharines, ON
L2M 5V6

Published in the United States
Crabtree Publishing
PMB 59051
350 Fifth Avenue, 59th Floor
New York, New York 10118

Published in the United Kingdom
Crabtree Publishing
Maritime House
Basin Road North, Hove
BN41 1WR

Published in Australia
Crabtree Publishing
3 Charles Street
Coburg North
VIC, 3058

CONTENTS

Mom wanted to talk. In fact, she had taken Meg to the mall to have the conversation. They had just found a funky pair of sandals that were perfect for the summer. Somehow Meg sensed her mom was nervous. Meg knew she was going to hear something she wouldn't like.

It came over lunch. When Meg finished her salad, her mom broke the news. She and Brian were getting married. Brian? Really? *What a geek,* Meg thought. *He wears the ugliest ties on the planet.* Plus, Brian had two kids of his own—two little second graders.

As far as Meg was concerned, her life was ruined. Dad was gone and now this. If there was anything else, she was going to stay with her grandma. At least there she'd have some privacy.

Meg felt she'd been pretty cool about her mother dating other men. Meg even babysat a couple of times so she could go out. But marriage? Meg drew the line there. If Dad didn't mind, maybe she could live with him and his new girlfriend. At least she'd have some peace and quiet.

Introduction
Mixing It Up

Meg will soon be part of a blended family. Blended families form when a parent of one family remarries into another family with children.

Most blended families usually need time to adjust to one another. This period of **transition** can take months or years. Merging two families under one roof can be challenging, but it can also be rewarding.

The adults in a blended family are normally excited about bringing everyone together. Each parent might be a little nervous, but in the end they want everything to work out for their children and for their new relationship. Sometimes the kids feel the same way. Other times, not so much.

Becoming part of a blended family can be very challenging. There will be big changes, new routines, new rules, and maybe even a new place to live. It can be overwhelming. It can be stressful. But, sometimes, it can also be great.

"When Mom and Dad got divorced, I thought it was the end of the world. How could Mom do this? How could Dad just walk away? I was angry. I was sad. We used to have such a happy life together. Now everything will change." Alanza, 12.

Chapter 1
The Big "D"

There are many reasons why parents find new spouses. A mom or dad might get remarried after a spouse dies or after a divorce. Regardless of the circumstances, parents often decide to remarry. More often than not, they marry partners with children of their own. When this happens, the two families must come together and share a life.

Feelings of anger, grief, powerlessness, confusion, and helplessness are common when families split up. If you feel that way, don't despair. You're not alone. Many marriages end in divorce.

Although not all parents remarry or find new partners, many do. Nearly one out of three people become part of a blended family once in their lifetime.

While blended families have their challenges, they can be exciting. You might have several new brothers and sisters to do things with. You might have a new set of grandparents. You might even get new pets.

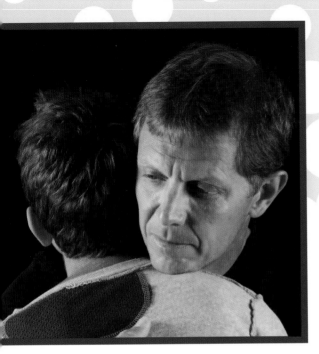

A divorce can leave you wondering "what's going to happen to me?"

By the Numbers

- The 2012 divorce rate in Canada was 40 percent, and in the United States, it was 46 percent.
- In the United States, 48 percent of first marriages will end in divorce, as will 46 percent of second marriages.

Sources: CBC and U.S. Census Bureau

No One Asked Me

It's not unusual to be the last to know that your parents are getting a divorce. Studies suggest that only about five percent of kids are included in this conversation.

Parents have their reasons for keeping a divorce to themselves at first. For example, they may not be absolutely sure if they're going to separate. Or, perhaps, they want to choose the best time to share the news with you and your siblings.

Whatever the reason, ending a marriage is never easy. Parents have to consider many things. They have to deal with their emotions, their financial situations, child-custody agreements, and many other difficult issues.

Age Matters

How you react to a divorce may depend on your age. Younger children will be saddened by the news of their parents' breakup. They may **grieve** openly. They may cry, feel sad, and wonder if their parents hate them. Younger children will often blame themselves for the situation.

As a result, it is common for young kids to lash out at friends or their siblings. Some might have nightmares. Others might develop health issues. Younger children might also pick the side of one parent over the other.

Preteen

Older children, such as preteens, may feel angry, sad, and anxious. They'll probably be mad at their parents and express this anger. They might also blame themselves. They might be afraid that both their mom and dad will forget them.

Preteens might bury themselves in schoolwork. They might have headaches or stomachaches from stress. They might swear, act out, or say things they don't mean. It's not unusual for preteens to want a lot of alone time. Sometimes it takes months to accept that their parents are ending their marriage.

Stress often accompanies divorce.

Teenagers

Teenagers might feel as if their parents are taking away their home. They might worry about what's going to happen to them. They might also pull away from their family and hang out more often with friends.

Many will blame their parents for ruining their lives. They might even side with their mother one day, and their father the next. They may even **vow** to never marry or have children of their own.

Many children think their parents' divorce is somehow their fault. Such guilt is normal, but not grounded in reality. Parents don't end marriages because of children; they end marriages because of their own problems.

In some families, children might feel a sense of relief, especially if they live in an abusive household. All these feelings and situations are normal. It may take time for them to pass. If you find the feelings too **overwhelming**, ask your parents if you can see a counselor. You can also talk to your doctor, a teacher, or a close friend.

It can be hard to watch your parents end their marriage. Sometimes you feel like you're to blame. You're not.

Blame Game

Expect to feel a lot of different emotions if your parents divorce. You'll likely spend a lot of time trying to figure out what's going to happen to you. Which parent will I live with? Will I have to change schools? Will I have to make new friends?

You'll want someone to blame. That someone will probably be your parents. You will feel scared and unsure about the future. You might find that some days you don't care what happens. Other days you will wish it would all just go away.

Divorce is hard on everyone. You might experience feelings of loneliness and fear after your parents split up.

Watching a parent walk out the door can be the worst feeling in the world. You feel helpless, alone, sad, and **abandoned**. Worst of all, there's a sense of betrayal. Parents don't intentionally want to make their kids' lives hard. It may sometimes feel that way, however.

"One of the things I disliked the most about having divorced parents was when I was little and had to go back and forth between my two parents. I always liked visiting both my parents, but on the last day before I would leave one's house, I'd be sad." Inez, 13.

Chapter 2
Healthy Families

Every family member, no matter their age, contributes to the **dynamics** of a family. Healthy families tend to have certain characteristics that keep the family bond tight. Some of those characteristics are listed below.

- Communication: Communication is one of the most important features of a healthy family. Good communication involves talking and listening. Healthy communication requires someone to say something, someone to hear it, think about it, and then respond.
- Trust: Knowing your mom and dad trust you to do the right thing will help build your self-esteem. Knowing that you can depend on your parents and any member of your family to be there for you during a crisis is a **critical** part of a trusting family relationship.
- Goal Setting: Goals can be as simple as washing the supper dishes before going to a movie, or as involved as being available on a Saturday to rake leaves. Goal setting brings a family together in a common purpose and strengthens its ties.

Talk it Out!

A person's cultural background influences how they interact with family members. Culture, which includes the beliefs, customs, and practices of a particular group of people, determines the type of conversations a child has with their parents, siblings, grandparents, and other relatives. Customs, which are passed from one generation to the next, will change as time goes on. Still, respecting customs are important to a family's dynamic.

What Did You Say?

Communication isn't always about what you say—it's about how you say things, including your tone and the volume of your voice.

Non-verbal communication is just as important as verbal communication. Hand gestures, facial expressions, grunting, body posture, or not saying anything at all can convey messages louder than words. To get along, be mindful of the non-verbal side of communication—it can say a lot.

Dinner is an ideal time to talk with your family. Family members can catch up on what's new, make plans, and discuss any issues.

No One's Listening

People cope in many ways during a divorce, including your parents. They may get **irritable** or be sad. Try these coping **strategies** if your parents are going through a divorce.

- Talk to your siblings. They're probably feeling the same as you.
- Talk to your grandparents.
- Teachers, counselors, clergy, or a family doctor can also help you understand the situation.
- Write in a journal, blog, or find an online help site.

Jotting down your feelings in a journal can often help you understand what is happening in your life.

The Upside

Positive things can happen during a divorce, too. You might become closer to your siblings and your friends. You might even become more of an understanding and mature person. Recognizing and understanding what your parents are dealing with is much different than liking the situation.

"I was bringing my ten-year-old son home and I pulled up in front of his mother's house. My son said, 'Daddy, I want to live with you when I'm 18.' My heart broke. 'Do you want to live with me now? We can tell the judge you want to do that.' He then replied, 'No, Mommy will get mad at me and hate me, and I don't want that.'" Frank, 36.

Chapter 3
In the Middle

Once upon a time, families consisted of a mom, a dad, and their children. **Sociologists** called these family units nuclear families. Nuclear families were once the most basic and universal of all family relationships.

This is not the case anymore. Change is inevitable. Unfortunately, when parents divorce, children are often caught in the middle. All these changes might mean a new house, a new school, new friends, and a new neighborhood. You might also find yourself with a new parent, a new bedroom, and new siblings. That's a ton of new stuff to get used to!

It's common to feel stressed, scared, and a bit confused. Maybe you're angry. Who can blame you? Change is difficult to deal with, especially when you're battling a number of other issues related to growing up. At times it can seem overwhelming.

The New Kid

No one likes to be the new kid in school. Being the new kid means a new classroom, new rules, new textbooks, and new teachers. Will you be able to make new friends? Will it be hard for you to stay in touch with your old friends?

Let's face it, reality bites sometimes, but there are things you can do to bite back.

- Check it out! Go online and see what the new school looks like before you move.
- Visit the new neighborhood if you can. Find the closest mall and pizza parlor. Map the bus routes. Pinpoint the library.
- See what kind of courses, after-school activities, and sports the school offers.
- Get one of your parents to drive you to the school and take a tour.
- Send an email to your new teachers and introduce yourself.

When you're the new kid in school, your world is often turned inside out.

The Financial Blues

You might also find yourself worried about the family finances. Mom never had to work before, and now she's looking for a job.

It's not unusual to worry about such things. Your parent might have to pay **alimony** to your other parent. You might have to move into an apartment or move in with other relatives. You need to prepare for and understand all these issues.

Coping with Custody

A custody agreement **mandated** by the courts is law. In other words, both your parents must follow the agreement. You also have to abide by a judge's decision.

Custody agreements can say where you spend the holidays and your vacations. Judges approve custody agreements to protect your interests and the interest of all **minor** children.

Custody agreements put in writing which parent has legal custody of you and your siblings. The agreements will also state visitation schedules; pick-up and drop-off locations; and decisions regarding your religious upbringing, education, and extracurricular activities.

Parents often reach custody agreements on their own. A judge still has to approve, or change, the agreement.

Special Occasions

Birthdays, holidays, and special occasions can be stressful, especially if your parents can't **compromise**. Even if your parents get along, you can often feel like a rag doll being pulled in too many directions.

Age makes a difference in how you handle the situation. Preteens might have strong feelings about who they want to spend special occasions with. They might become angry and cry, or lash out at their parents because they don't agree with their decisions.

As a teen, you might be so involved with your own life that you might see it as an **imposition** to be told where you're spending your time. You might not even care. Then again, you may feel angry and frustrated at the lack of control you have over your life.

If it's too much to handle, try talking to your parents. Tell them you're having a hard time. Say exactly what you feel. Don't yell. Don't argue.

Choosing between parents can make you feel alone.

20

Empathy

Empathy is important to think about, too. Try to put yourself in your parents' shoes. Ask these questions:

- When was the last time I spent a special occasion with this parent?
- How important is it to my parent that I attend?
- Will I hurt someone's feelings if I don't go?
- Is there a compromise we can agree to?
- What do I want to do?
- How can I communicate honestly and openly while still being respectful?

Compromise is often the best solution in deciding where you will spend special occasions, such as birthdays.

By the Numbers

In the United States, more than 36 percent of women and 38.8 percent of men between the ages of 20 to 24 are divorced.

Source: Centers for Disease Control, National Survey of Family Growth

Something that was hard for both my stepdad and me was the 'you're-not-my-dad' card I would pull on him. In return, he'd say 'you're not my kid.' One time he gave my brother a donut in front of me. When I asked if he had one for me, he looked at me and said, 'you're not my kid.' Jo, 16.

Chapter 4
The New Family

Going through a divorce is pretty tough, but the emotional roller coaster can start all over again when one, or both, of your parents decide to remarry.

You might have a long list of new questions that you want answered. Where are we going to live? How will I fit in? Where will your other parent fit in? Will I have to take orders from my stepparent? What are his kids like? Will I like them? Will they like me? Will I have to share a room?

Parents sometimes decide to live together with a new partner instead of getting married. Regardless, two families coming together under one roof can cause a lot of tension and feelings of uncertainty.

Putting the Step in Family

About 75 percent of divorced couples will remarry. Of these marriages, 65 percent will have blended families of various combinations. That means over half of these families have children and parents that are not **biologically** related.

Of course, those statistics do not count the 25 percent of blended families with couples that are living together who are not married. Altogether, about one third of all the people in families are a stepchild, stepmother, stepfather, or stepsibling.

You might become jealous or angry when you're tossed in the middle of a blended family. You're afraid because your mom or dad won't have any time for you. You're worried because you don't know what it will be like to live with a new set of brothers, sisters, pets, and who knows what else.

There is no one way to cope with a newly formed stepfamily.

Expect some tense moments when two families mix.

Death of a Parent

Following the death of a parent the surviving spouse may want to remarry. Having a new stepparent fill the lost parent's place can often set off a lot of emotional grief. Many people deal with grief in stages, which are described below.

The process of grieving over a lost parent is long and complicated. In time, you will accept the death and begin to move on.

- Denial: Denial is the first step in the grieving process. When a loved one dies, your first response is to deny the loss and want to be alone.

- Anger: After the initial pain, you will become angry.

- Bargaining: Bargaining helps ease the pain of loss. It usually goes something like this: "If we'd only got treatment earlier she'd be alive."

- Depression: This feeling prepares you for accepting the loss.

- Acceptance: The final stage is acceptance, which is sometimes confused with depression. During this period you will come to accept the death and prepare to move on.

These stages don't always happen in order, and some happen faster than others. Sometimes we think we're over a death or loss of a loved one, only to have intense emotions resurface.

Yours, Mine, and Theirs

Life in your new home can be pretty awkward at first, especially if one or more of your new stepsiblings is of the opposite sex. You might be used to running around the house in your underwear.

Now what? Suddenly, you're confronted by a stepsister who uses tampons, or a stepbrother who is going through **puberty**. As such, there might be some awkward and embarrassing moments, and perhaps, insensitive remarks. No one likes to share their private lives.

As time goes on, a new routine will work itself out. If you have issues, talk it out. Communicate and be honest, but try not to be unkind.

Figuring out which TV show to watch can often be difficult with a new stepsibling.

Coping Strategies

It can be challenging to live with people you're not familiar with. You might argue. You might want to shut down completely. There are better ways to handle such stressful situations.

- Use "I" instead of "you" when speaking with a stepsibling or stepparent. "You" sounds as if you're trying to start an argument or point the finger of blame. "I" expresses how you feel about a situation.
- Listen to the other person's point of view. He or she might have something important to say or a solution to the problem.
- Be respectful. Don't insult people, or their ideas.
- Explain the problem to your parents. They might have good suggestions or solutions.
- Take a deep breath and ask yourself why you're mad. Sometimes when you're unhappy you lash out at other people who have nothing to do with the situation.
- If you cannot cope with a new stepbrother or stepsister, ask your parent if you can speak with a therapist. Sometimes an **unbiased** viewpoint works wonders.

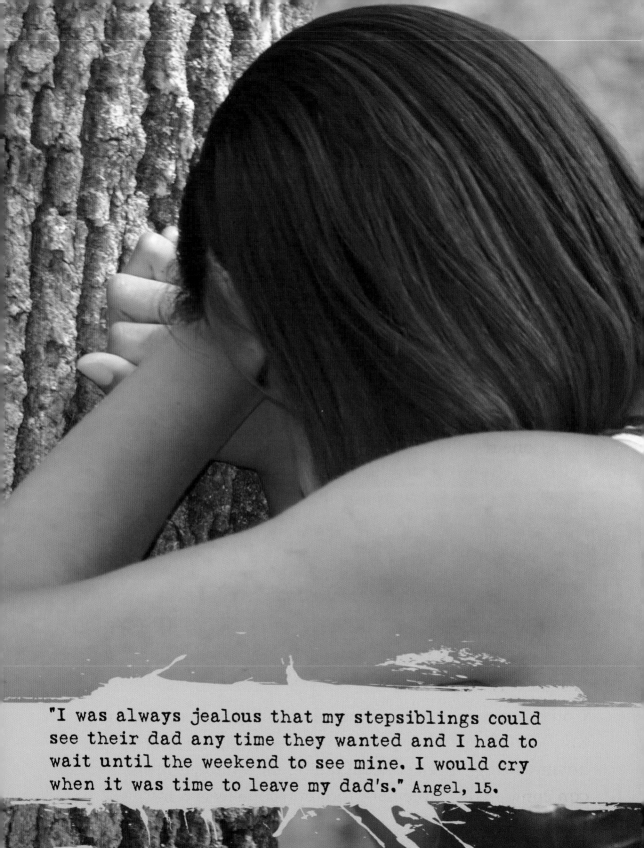

"I was always jealous that my stepsiblings could see their dad any time they wanted and I had to wait until the weekend to see mine. I would cry when it was time to leave my dad's." Angel, 15.

Chapter 5
"You're Not My Mom!"

You gave it your best shot, or so you think. You've tried everything to get along with your new stepfamily, but it's just not working. Why can't things go back to the way they were?

Problems can erupt when you put a group of individuals under one roof. If you're finding that the situation is getting worse, ask yourself what's really bugging you. When you figure it out, speak up.

Talking is the key to a happy family life. Speak with your biological parent and voice your concerns. Tell your parent that you miss them and you are finding it difficult to spend time with them. Suggest setting aside one day each week to spend time together. If you feel comfortable, invite your stepparent to join the conversation as well.

Compromise is essential if people are to get along. Call a family meeting. Air your **grievances**. Maybe someone else is having a similar issue. See if you, your parent, and stepparent can come to an agreement that everyone feels is fair.

Jumbled Feelings

It's hard to care about another person's feelings or opinions when your own feelings are hurt. Yet, caring about another person can go a long way to solve a problem.

Treating people with respect shows that you value another person's opinion. If you want to be treated respectfully, you must earn it. Refrain from cursing or bad-mouthing your stepparent, or stepbrothers or sisters. Be positive. Try to understand their feelings. Ask that they try to understand your feelings, too. Try to find something positive in your parents' new relationship.

Toxic Behavior

Manipulating and lying is an unhealthy way to solve your problems. If you cope by using drugs or alcohol, you may be putting your life at risk. Look for other options. Try to find a way to gain some perspective instead of abusing substances.

Clearing the air with your parents can make life in a blended family a lot less stressful.

30

Abusive Situations

Children expect parents and stepparents to protect them. Abuse is a clear violation of that trust. Abuse can take many forms, some of which include:

- Verbal Abuse: Verbal abuse occurs in a variety of ways. A stepparent might **degrade** you in front of other people. They hurl insults at you, or tell hurtful jokes. They call you names or humiliate you. They might even blame, accuse, and criticize.
- Psychological Abuse: Does your stepparent ignore your feelings? Do they threaten you? Do they always control what you do, whom you talk to, and where you go? These are all signs of psychological abuse. Psychological abuse can also include leaving younger children unsupervised; making kids feel stupid and useless; talking in inappropriate ways, or putting kids in dangerous situations.
- Physical Abuse: There are many forms of physical abuse. Pushing, slapping, beating, kicking, and choking are all forms of physical abuse.
- Sexual Abuse: There are many types of sexual abuse, but it usually includes forcing someone to perform a sexual act.

If your parent brings a stepparent into the home that is abusive to you, your siblings, or your stepsiblings, you need to seek help right away. If it feels wrong, it probably is. Tell your parent. Tell a teacher. Call a cop. Phone a helpline.

"Having a blended family gives you a different outlook on life. You are able to see things from different angles. My stepmom came into my life over five years ago. It was hard at first, but now we get along just great. I've come to care about her a lot." Sierra, 13.

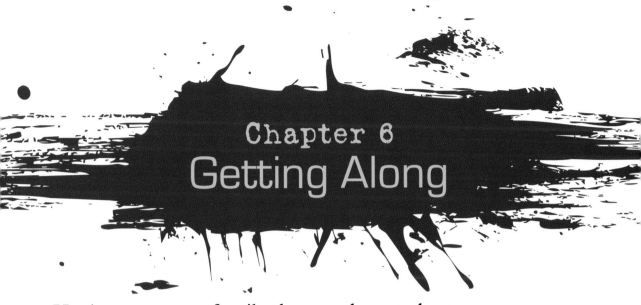

Chapter 6
Getting Along

Having a new stepfamily does not have to be a bad thing. Some have benefits that traditional families don't offer.

With a blended family usually comes a new social circle of friends and relatives. There are more people to interact with, and more things you can do as a group. Blended families also offer new opportunities to find someone you can trust and talk with when you need to unload.

Blended families can include people from different cultural backgrounds. You may celebrate new holidays, travel to different places, and even learn a new language.

If you think about it, there's a huge opportunity to learn new things, meet new people, and experience a new way of doing things. In a way, it's kind of exciting to have a big family—there's always something to do!

Happy Again

It may have been a long time since your mom and dad divorced. They've changed now that they have someone new in their lives. They smile more, they're easier to get along with, and there's more laughter in the house. The world is a nicer place with a happy parent.

New Arrivals

Have you ever wandered around the house wishing you had someone to talk to or go out with? A lot of kids in blended families say it's great having stepsiblings to do things with. You can learn a lot from stepbrothers and sisters. You can become friends, especially if you're the same age. You might find that younger stepsiblings look up to you for guidance and see you as a role model.

One day, your parent and stepparent may decide to have a baby together. New arrivals can be exciting. Babies can be a source of joy for everyone. They can also help pull your blended family closer together.

When your parents have new people in their lives, you might find they are a lot happier and easier to get along with.

Taking Responsibility

A big part of getting along with your new family is being realistic. Not everything is going to be easy, but it's not all going to be hard, either. It's all what you make it.

If you go into the situation expecting the worst, then that's probably what's going to happen. Yet, if you keep an open mind, keep the lines of communication open, and be respectful of every member of your new family, things will have a better chance of working out.

Maintaining a healthy relationship between family members is your responsibility, too. You can do it if you care about making the new living situation work. It might take some effort. It might mean compromising when you don't want to. In the end, you can do it.

"I Like You"

You may discover that you actually like your new stepparent. You might feel as though you are betraying one of your biological parents.

Caring about your stepparent does not mean you care less for your biological parent.

It might take a bit of time, but you may find that you love your new stepparent. You get along well and do things together.

"Coming from a blended family has both its ups and downs, just as any other family does. However, when change first sets in, it can be somewhat difficult to get used to. That's because everyone has a different standard of how to raise children." Aasma, 32.

Chapter 7
Seeking Help

You have a lot going on in your life. There's school, puberty, and other emotional stuff. It's a lot to handle, even in a perfect world. Now add a new family situation. Who can blame you for feeling a little overwhelmed?

Negative emotions can be overpowering. Anger can consume you. Guilt and shame can put you into a spiral of depression. If things are too much to handle, and you find yourself down in the dumps, it could be time to ask for help.

It's not unusual that new stepparents may have different ideas about what's right or wrong, or what's appropriate and what's not. Ask your mom or dad what he or she expects of you in the new family dynamic. If you have an opportunity, talk with your new stepparent. Ask about his or her expectations and rules. Tell them what you're used to, and if a compromise is needed, hash it out without getting angry.

Love and Loyalty

It's normal to wonder if your biological parent's love for you will stop and be given to the new stepparent and stepsiblings. Try to remember that your parent is also transitioning into a new life.

You may like your new stepfamily, but still have conflicting feelings and loyalties to your biological parents and siblings. You may also think that your siblings or parent get along better with your stepsiblings. You might enjoy spending time with one parent as opposed to the other.

If you feel that you are being disloyal to a parent or sibling, or you feel you're not being included in the family, talk it out. Keep the lines of communication open and strong.

How to Cope

Learning to control intense negative emotions can help you remain calm during a crisis. The next time you get angry or frustrated, try some of these techniques and see if the situation improves:

- Keeping a journal helps you think clearly. Once the words are on paper, the situation that made you angry may not seem as important or as hard to handle.
- Talking to a person who is going through a similar situation is also helpful.
- Share your feelings with your mom or dad. Let him or her know what's bothering you, no matter how silly it may sound.
- Understanding what makes you angry can help you deal with your emotions and gain control.

Be Mature

There are always two sides to any argument. If you feel there is an argument in the making, stop talking for a moment and listen to what the other person is saying.

Think about what you want to say. Screaming, crying, pouting, and stomping will not get you anywhere. You need to build **credibility**. You need to show the other person that you are mature and should be respected.

Stepsibling Rivalry

Integrating into a new family can lead to rivalry with your stepsiblings. For example, you might have been the oldest in the family, but now you have an older stepsister. Or maybe you're feeling the sting of not being your mom's favorite anymore because there's a younger stepsibling taking up her time.

Conflict is common in all families. The best way to deal with any conflict is to talk it out. Remember to be calm and respectful to everyone. Be tolerant and compassionate about the other person's feelings. In the end, you might find they are more understanding of you.

Things will get better when you build credibility among your stepsiblings.

Helping a Friend

Do you have a friend that is going through a rough time with a new family, and you're not sure what to say or do? A sympathetic ear can help.

Just listening and being supportive can reassure a friend that he or she is not alone. Sometimes an encouraging word is helpful. Sometimes your friend needs more help than you can give. If you think your friend's problem is becoming destructive or heading in an unhealthy direction, it's time to suggest other options, such as talking to a counselor or teacher. If your friend refuses, go to an adult you trust. Let your friend know that you still care and are there for him or her.

It can be heartbreaking to see a friend who is hurting. But how can you make it better? Sometimes just being there makes a big difference.

What if Nothing Works?

You've talked to your parent and stepparent, yet you still can't get along with your blended family. You're miserable and you don't know where to turn. Maybe it's time to seek professional help. Asking for help may be hard to do. You might feel you don't want to bother anyone with your problems. Maybe you feel that if you ask for help you'll embarrass yourself.

You don't have to handle your problems alone.

Recognizing you need support is a sign of strength and maturity. You can't handle every situation alone. Living in a situation that is making you feel terrible is not healthy.

So, you have to find a person who you trust and who can listen without judging. Ask your parent to find a therapist for you. If that's not an option, talk to an aunt, uncle, or grandparent. Don't wait for someone to come to you. Be **proactive**. Talk to a member of the clergy, call a helpline, or ask a teacher or a school counselor for help.

What Do I Say?

What do you talk about when you're in therapy? That's a good question. The short answer is "it depends." It depends on your situation. It depends on what you want to talk about.

You might want to ask your therapist if your conversations will be kept private, or will he or she discuss them with your parents. In some cases, the law says parents have a right to know what a therapist and their child discuss. However, the laws are different in many areas.

It is often good for your parent and stepparent to know what you and your therapist are discussing. Talk to your therapist and find out what the ground rules are.

Asking for help can be hard to do, but it's well worth it.

Once you are in treatment, you might find it hard to speak about private matters. Regardless, your therapist needs to know why you are feeling what you're feeling—no matter how difficult it is to discuss.

Like a Ping-Pong Ball

You now realize your dad is still your dad and your mom is still your mom. Still, you feel like a ping-pong ball, always bouncing between families. If you are feeling overwhelmed, confused, and frustrated, try some of these coping strategies:

- Relax. Breathe. Try to understand why you are really upset.
- Plan. Keep a backpack or suitcase with your schoolbooks and other necessities. That way you're always prepared.
- Communicate. If you have a major test coming up, maybe it's best to stay put and study. Talk to your parents about your concerns.
- Be flexible. If for some reason you can't stay with your parent because something comes up in their lives, don't take it personally.

Hot Topics
Q&A

What's the difference between a blended family and a stepfamily?

A: There is no difference. The term "blended" is now the preferred term. Many people believe there is a negative association with the word "stepfamily."

Can I choose who I want to live with when my parents divorce?

A: What happens generally depends on how old you are. The older you are, the more a judge will consider your request.

Am I a bad person for wanting to be with my stepdad more than my father?

A: No, you're not a bad person, you're an honest person. Maybe you have a bad history with your father, or feel that he doesn't understand or love you as your stepdad understands or loves you.

My stepmom is always badmouthing my mom. How can I make her stop?

A: Talk to your dad about the situation and tell him how it makes you feel. Ask him to talk to your stepmom. Maybe your stepmother doesn't realize how her words impact you.

I see my stepfather hitting my brother. What should I do?

A: If you see or think that a stepparent is being abusive, call the police, talk to a teacher, a counselor, or call a helpline. It is not acceptable to abuse anyone.

We have a great blended family. Both my mom's new husband and my dad's wife are great. I get along with them and all my stepbrothers and sisters. Is that normal?

A: Each blended family situation is different. It's wonderful when everyone gets along. Although most blended families need time to adjust, some get along right from the start.

Now that I'm living in a blended family, we're starting all these new traditions. Am I wrong for not liking them?

A: Your parent and stepparent are very smart people. One way to make a blended family feel more like a family is to establish new traditions. Give it time, you might enjoy them.

Other Resources

There is limited information on blended families directed specifically to adolescents and teens. However, there is a lot of information available for parents and families. Some is reliable, some is not. Here are some sources you may find helpful. The Web sites have information significant in Canada and the United States. Telephone numbers are good in either Canada or the United States, but not both. If you do call a number outside of your area, the helpline will refer you to a number in your area.

In Canada

Stepfamily Foundation of Alberta
http://www.stepfamily.ca/frames.htm
This site offers information on how to cope with divorce; moving between homes; effective communication; and much more.

The Step and Blended Family Institute
http://www.stepinstitute.ca/what_we_do.php
The Step and Blended Family Institute provides advice and programs on blended families to those living in Southern Ontario.

Families Change
http://teens.familieschange.ca/
A site specifically designed for teens to help them
deal with divorce, changing families, and figuring
out coping strategies.

In the United States

KidsHealth.org
http://kidshealth.org/
This site provides information for teens, young kids,
and adults about family and health issues.

YMCA
http://www.ymca.net/healthy-family-home/
The YMCA offers advice on what it takes to make a
healthy family life.

National Stepfamily Resource Center
http://www.stepfamilies.info/
The National Stepfamily Resource Center's Web site offers
information about stepfamilies. There is also a page of
questions for children and adults.

Hotlines

KidsHelpPhone.ca
1-800-668-6868

Youth Crisis Line
1-800-448-4663

Family Violence Helpline
1-800-222-2000

Glossary

abandoned Leave somebody behind for others to look after

alimony Financial support to an ex-spouse

biologically Connected by a direct genetic relationship

compromise A settlement of differences

credibility Ability to inspire belief or trust

critical Tending to find fault with somebody or something

degrade To put down

dynamics The relationships of power between people in a group

empathy Understanding another's feelings

grievances Complaints

grieve Feel sorrow

imposition A burden

irritable Easily annoyed

mandated A formal order by a court

minor A person who has not yet attained legal age

non-verbal Little or no use of speech

overwhelming to upset or overpower

proactive Acting in anticipation of future changes

puberty The stage where the human body becomes capable of reproducing

sociologists Scientists who study society and social relationships

strategies A plan of action

transition Process or period in which something undergoes a change

unbiased Not holding a particular point of view; fair

vow A promise

Index